IMAGES OF ENGLAND

THE LONGDENDALE VALLEY

IMAGES OF ENGLAND

THE LONGDENDALE VALLEY

MARGARET BUXTON

TEMPUS

Frontispiece: The Longdendale Valley.

First published 2004

Tempus Publishing Limited
The Mill, Brimscombe Port,
Stroud, Gloucestershire, GL5 2QG
www.tempus-publishing.com

British Library Cataloguing in Publication Data.
A catalogue record for this book is available from the British Library.

ISBN 0 7524 3288 5

Typesetting and origination by Tempus Publishing Limited.
Printed in Great Britain.

Contents

Harry Buxton the photographer in 1969.

Acknowledgements

It was the collection of photographs taken by my late father Harry Buxton (1908–1983) which was the inspiration for this book. For most of his life he was a professional photographer and he never left his home in Hadfield without a camera. During the war he was a police photographer based at Glossop.

   Often as a child, the beautiful Longdendale Valley was the place where we walked, identifying wild flowers and watching the steam trains. Sometimes we would drive around the reservoirs and marvel at the wonderful panoramic views. My parents were married at Mottram church and my grandmother lived for many years in the village after moving from the old farming community in Hattersley. I spent many happy hours on the swings and roundabouts next to her home in Mottram and I still have other relatives in the area. I am grateful that my father helped me to appreciate the beauty around us and for wanting to preserve and share the many memories which these photographs evoke.

Introduction

In the Domesday survey of 1086, when a man named Lingulf held the land, Longdendale was listed as Lange de Nedele, the Long Valley between Mottram and Saltersbrook a distance of about ten miles. It was described as waste, unpastured woodland and fit only for hunting and valued at only forty shillings. It was part of the Royal Forest of the Peak and so the King reserved it as his hunting right because wildcat, otter, deer and wild boar all roamed. Giant footprints were once found in the Rhodes Wood area and are thought to be from a creature more than 330 million years ago. Man has occupied Longdendale for more than 8,000 years in spite of the dense woodland of native species like oak, birch and pine. Many have left their mark in the Longdendale Valley. The Stone Age hunters left behind implements and flints; and arrowheads from the Bronze Age been found near a natural mound named Torside Castle. The Celts brought their iron-working skills, customs and superstitions. The Romans built a fort to house auxiliary troops at Melandra on a site overlooking the river Etherow near Glossop and also one on the western end of the Longdendale Valley named Edrotalia. Longdendale provided a route for them to march to another fort at Brough in Yorkshire. A Roman road also ran over the moors from Tintwistle Knarr to Highstones. A Saxon king is said to have invaded the valley to fight the Celts with warriors from Yorkshire, the casualties are thought to be buried in mounds between Woodhead and Torside. It was the Anglo-Saxons who cleared the sites for our modern day villages. Most of these follow the Saxon custom of naming places after nature, thus Arnfield meant 'eagle's head' and Crowden meant 'corner of the valley'. In the Middle Ages the Earls of Chester arranged the county boundaries to preserve the salt routes, so Longdendale became known as 'a finger of Cheshire pointing into Yorkshire.' Salters Road and Salters Brook mark the boundary between the two counties and traders would walk past the summit mark at 'Ladies Cross' and proceed to the markets over the border. Other parts of the Royal Forest were named Hopedale and Campagne. Each division held a court every forty days and Longdendale's was held in either Glossop or Charlesworth. Longdendale is usually associated with the villages on the Cheshire side of the River Etherow (i.e. Tintwistle, Hollingworth and Mottram) but by the eleventh century the name referred to the whole valley of the Etherow and included land in both Derbyshire and Cheshire.

The river Etherow is carried from its source beyond Woodhead near Saltersbrook, down the valley to its junction with Glossop Brook. During the Ice Age the valley, being on the edge of the ice-covered Pennines with extensive snowfalls, formed many overflow channels from the melt water. The alternate freezing and melting of the water on rocks produced many landslips that now give the valley its character. Boulder clay is very prominent in the lower valley extending as far as Torside. Many years later Mottram church was built, from grit stone, overlooking the villages and dominating the skyline.

Longdendale today forms the upper part of the Etherow valley, which runs between two and three hundred metres below the summit of the South Pennine Hills. William de Neville was the first Lord of Longdendale when it encompassed the medieval Manors of Godley, Hattersley, Hollingworth, Matley, Newton, Staley, Tintwistle and Werneth. Legend has it that Robin Hood was a frequent visitor to the valley and that the forests were so dense that squirrels could leap between trees all the way from Mottram to Woodhead.

Industrialists saw the potential of the River Etherow Valley and the biggest civil engineering site ever seen, started in the valley with the construction of reservoirs. Two regulated the flow of water to power the mills and the other three were to be used for drinking water as the natural spring water in areas like Spring Gardens and Fountain Street in Manchester was dwindling. The reservoirs were described as the largest expanse of water on the face of the globe. The textile industry, which had started in homes in the eighteenth century, moved into the new mills beside the reservoirs making Longdendale a thriving cotton valley. In the nineteenth century, the railway companies also discovered that Woodhead at the top of the valley was the easiest place to cross the Pennine hills. In 1838 the largest railway tunnel of the day was started at Woodhead. George Stevenson and Isambard Kingdom Brunel had both tendered for the job but George Vignoles won the contract and later Joseph Locke joined the elite engineers. There were many casualties due to accident and disease and the burials of the victims took place at Woodhead and Tintwistle. As the valley began to thrive, communities grew and better conditions developed. The deer and boar have long since gone but the valley is still a haven for wildlife, curlews, lapwings and birds of prey make up some of the resident bird life as well as winter visitors like the redwings and fieldfares and in the spring the cuckoo returns. Blue hares have also been seen on higher ground especially sporting their white coats in winter. The Coat of Arms for Longdendale is based on the family arms of the Hollingworths of Hollingworth Old Hall.

The 1991 Census revealed that the population of Longdendale was 10,581 but still six had no inside WC, five had no bath or shower and 653 had no central heating. Today well over ten thousand vehicles a day pound the A628 through Mottram, Hollingworth, Tintwistle, Crowden and Woodhead on their way to Yorkshire, making life very difficult for so many residents. After much debate a relief road is to be made to alleviate the constant congestion particularly on Mottram Moor.

Take a look now down the Valley of Longdendale as seen in days gone by and revel in those reminders of the days of steam and waterpower and be thankful that this delightful area is still accessible to us all.

M.M. Buxton
June 2004

one

Woodhead

Woodhead in January 1963. Woodhead gets its name from the Wooded Hill at the head of the dense wood that once existed here. The source of the River Etherow is high up in moorland and flows down the Longdendale Valley to Woolley Bridge near Hadfield and then on to Marple Bridge where it joins the River Goyt, eventually becoming the River Mersey. In 1793 before the arrival of the mills, there were salmon in the Etherow. Over the years there has always been mystery regarding lights that are seen in the night sky on the moors near Shining Clough Moss and close to the Woodhead Tunnels. The very first direct railway between Manchester and Sheffield was known as the Sheffield, Ashton-under-Lyne & Manchester line and was opened in sections. The first part was from Manchester to Godley near Hyde and opened in 1841. The line through to Sheffield was only possible with the building of the first railway tunnel at Woodhead, which was opened in 1845. Workmen's cottages, stables, magazines for storing gunpowder and four miles of cart roads across the moors also had to be built. Over 157 tins of gunpowder were used for blasting and an incredible amount of water had to be pumped out during the six years that the first tunnel was under construction. There were frequent accidents and in 1849 cholera swept through the workmen's families. It was thought that it spread from Ashton where the navvies went drinking.

Woodhead station, *c.* 1950. On the right is the booking office. Above the two old railway tunnels built between 1939 and 1852 are some village houses and the tunnel observation tower is on the skyline.

A steam train emerges into Woodhead in around 1934 giving an indication of conditions suffered by the drivers in the tunnels. The first tunnel had only a single track and it soon became congested so a second was started in 1847 but cholera claimed the lives of twenty-eight workers in 1849 and it took about another three years to complete.

Inside the booking office in 1949. Over eighty trains, mainly carrying coal, passed each way through the tunnels. In 1936 LNER approved a scheme for the electrification of the Manchester to Sheffield lines. Before the third tunnel was built, the booking office and station house were demolished (*c.* 1950) to make way for a new track.

The railway navvies disliked the long tunnels and being very superstitious they erected gargoyles on the walls to ward off evil spirits.

Right: A lion was placed in the centre of the two portals on the western side of the tunnels.

Below: The start of the third Woodhead tunnel, *c.*1949. On the right is photographer Harry Buxton holding his son Stuart with Uncles William and Bennett Buxton, centre, and workers in front of the new tunnel. The spoil was used to fill in a ravine near Dunford Bridge at the eastern end of the tunnel.

Excavating the rock at the start of the new tunnel in June 1949. In the inset to the left, workmen in a bucket are descending a hole that becomes the 480 feet deep shaft to start the pilot tunnel near Dunford.

In May 1951 and 467 feet below ground the aptly named Mr J.C.L. Train (centre), watched by other rail officials, fired the final shot of explosive to break through the last rock to link the tunnelling from both sides. All present are decked out in wellingtons, hard hats and protective coats but it is surprising to see that the man at the front right was smoking.

Workers from the east and west sides of the tunnel greeted each other as the final break through was completed in May 1951. The third Woodhead tunnel, three miles and sixty-six yards in length, had been successfully cut.

By October 1953 the construction of the new tunnel was completed and at a cost of approximately four and a half million pounds. Watched by a train spotter, the final stage of installing the overhead electricity was finished in 1954. The redundant old tunnels were then used to carry power cables for the national grid.

The third Woodhead tunnel was lined with Portland stone, had electric lighting every 132 feet and emergency telephones installed in recesses every 660 feet. The phones were linked to new signal boxes at both Woodhead and Dunford. A special train bedecked with flags brought dignitaries, the national press and television cameras to Woodhead for the opening ceremony on 3 June 1954. Many people watched from the steep banking below the A628, including two small children from Hadfield (the author and her brother) who were granted a half day off school to watch the historic event and to see their father as he emerged from the gleaming locomotive to take photographs, including this one. This great achievement of civil engineering was undertaken by J.I. Campbell (civil engineer), Sir William Halcrow & Partners (consulting engineers), and Balfour Beatty & Company Ltd (civil engineering contractors). The locomotive 26020 and details of its history can now be seen at the National Railway Museum in York.

Alan Lennox-Boyd MP and Minister for Transport and Civil Aviation in 1954 performed the official opening ceremony of the tunnel.

The new platform and signal box at Woodhead station in 1954 showing the realigned track for the approach to the new tunnel.

Sadly, almost thirty years later in 1981, British Rail closed the line. The Longdendale Trail was created for cyclists, walkers and horses on the route of the old track between Hadfield and Woodhead. The author of this book stood by the closed tunnels in the 1990s shortly before discussions about re-opening the line for freight, took place.

Mr Alvin Willis and his dog Jack are seen in this faded old photograph outside the Angel Inn that stood near Nine Holes Bridge at Woodhead. When it was demolished in around 1920, the spirits licence was transferred to the Crown Inn, which stood near to the tunnels, and then also became known as the Angel. Tunnel workers were paid every nine weeks, often partly in beer tokens!

The main road at Woodhead (A628), the road to Huddersfield (A616) and the turn off to Holmfirth (A6024) have always been notorious for accidents due to the harsh weather and the dangerous bends. In 1951 a coach from the Olive Branch public house in Ashton crashed through a wall on the Holme Moss Road.

The George & Dragon Inn at the 'Devil's Elbow' junction. The building to the left was known as Saunders Cross House and was a place of Christian worship. One time landlord Fred Boley used to sell snuff to his customers and was reputed to substitute dried horse manure if it ran out! You could also weigh yourself as you entered the pub.

The inn closed in 1961 and landlady Mrs Annie Bagshaw (right) marked the occasion. Her husband used to greet hikers jovially with the words, 'Come in lads, I'm George and t'dragon's in t'kitchen'. The Australian Cricket Team visited in 1934 and 1938. Old documents were found in the walls in 1950, listing all the stagecoach stops between London and York.

St James' chapel in 1964, was founded in about 1487, for the people of Woodhead and Crowden. Edmund Shaa from Mottram left money to pay for its priest. The Irish navvies who died in accidents whilst working in the tunnels are buried here. The ashes of local lady Mary Earnshaw Buckley, who was a missionary to British Columbia, were scattered here.

'Sermons Sunday' at St James chapel in August 1939. About fifty people regularly attended and when they no longer had their own clergyman, services were officiated by vicars from Mottram church. In recent years, services have been quite rare but in 2003 it was the venue for a service of Christmas carols and readings.

The newly-wed Mr and Mrs Fazackerly left the church after their wedding at St James' chapel, Woodhead under an arch of hockey sticks, c. 1945. The chapel was lit with oil lamps and the porch was added in 1924 as a memorial to those who died in the First World War. In 1912 many gravestones on the floors were covered over and later wooden benches replaced the pews.

two

Crowden

A VIEW DOWN THE VALLEY FROM CROWDEN.

The Longdale Valley from Crowden.

The name Crowden is derived from Crow Dene meaning 'valley of crows' or 'corner of the valley.' The 256-mile long Pennine Way Path, from Edale in Derbyshire to Yetholm in Scotland, passes through Crowden. With Bleaklow on the south side and Black Hill on the north side, the Youth Hostel and campsite serve as welcome resting-places. The Youth Hostel was opened in 1965. The words, 'I've camped out at Crowden....' from the Manchester Rambler's song by Ewan McColl, highlighted the area. Cottages known as Brick Row were built in the village in the 1900s to house railway workers. Two small stones set in a wall near Crowden mark the site where two children lost their lives in a fire in 1854. Their father James Forshaw was a sub contractor for Mr Taylor at Arnfield Reservoir in Tintwistle.

WOODHEAD STATION

WOODHEAD ARCHES

PHOTO BY T.R. THOMPSON HADFIELD

A MERRY XMAS 1907

WOODHEAD CHURCH

SWEET IS THE MEMORY OF ABSENT FRIENDS

VILLAGE POSTMAN

CROWDEN VILLAGE

Souvenir of CROWDEN

VALE HOUSE HADFIELD

A collection of postcards and greeting cards depicting scenes from Woodhead and Crowden which were sent out far and wide in the early twentieth century. A cyclist poses outside St James' chapel before its porch was added and other buildings are shown long before their demise.

The Commercial Inn on the left was knocked down in the mid 1920s and is still an open stretch of land today. Relatives of Glynis Reeve ran it in the early days of the last century.

The row of cottages on the right of centre in this view later became the Youth Hostel. The vicarage, the vicarage cottage and a pair of semi-detached houses are some of the few private houses that remain in the village today. Many of the farms that once stood in Crowden were demolished or became submerged under the waters of the reservoirs.

These cottages were once Kidfield Paper Mill seen here after a great flood when much devastation was caused, *c.* 1912. Phillip and Christian Evans, who ran clay pigeon shooting near Bleaklow (known locally as the 'Boar Shoot') and Walter Woodleigh were amongst those who lived here.

Crowden Hall the manor house of the local gentry, 1924. The Tudor-style mansion was built in 1692 for the Hadfield family who were also known as 'Hatfield' and regarded as the squires of Crowden until they left in the 1830s. The initials over the door THED refer to Thomas Hadfield the Lord of the Manor. The broadcaster and author Melvyn Bragg wrote a book entitled *The Maid of Buttermere* which traces the life and downfall of Mr John Hadfield who was eventually hanged for fraud on the gallows at Carlisle jail. In 1997 the Bland family from Quiet Shepherd Farm, once a seventeenth century inn four miles from Tintwistle, applied to move their sheep to land belonging to the hall. This was to save their sheep going to Staffordshire each winter to prevent over grazing farmland owned by North West Water.

Opposite above: The rifle range used by the local Territorial Army, on the moors above Crowden. Cllr Vic Fazackerley, seen here, retired in 1962 after thirty years as its warden. Born in 1898, he served with the Lancashire Fusiliers 1915-1923, received the Award of Merit in 1943 by the GOC ack-ack command and the BEM in 1961. Mr J. Kirk succeeded him.

Opposite below: A commanding view of the valley from Crowden Rifle Range in the 1930s with the shooting targets in the centre. Farms are dotted about the valley and beyond is the Woodhead and Crowden cricket pitch with Crowden Hall to the left near the water of the reservoir. The cricket pitch later became a campsite.

Inside Crowden Hall looking towards the village and across the valley to Bleaklow.

Sadly Crowden Hall, with its ornate fireplaces, was demolished in around 1935 by the Water Authority.

Above: In October 1951 the main road was blocked for hours by a burning lorry that was carrying seven tons of paraffin. On the right (inset) is the driver Mr John Brackstone who managed to jump clear of the conflagration.

Left: A lorry accident at Crowden in July 1956. Apparently a wasp entered the cab and distracted the driver, Mr John Gilbert Croft causing him to collide with another lorry driven by Frank Holden of Mossley. Stone Row cottages at the top of the photograph were later turned into the Youth Hostel which was officially opened in June 1965 by Mr Fred Willey the Minister for Land & Natural Resources.

Left: In January 1963, driver Mr L.J. Parker from Audenshaw had a lucky escape when his articulated lorry plunged eighty feet from Crowden to a culvert running besides Rhodeswood Reservoir. Across the water can be seen Crowden station and houses on the Derbyshire side of The Longdendale Valley.

Below: The signalman on duty at Crowden station on this day in around 1957 was Tom Rowbottom from Tintwistle who worked at many of the boxes on the Hadfield to Woodhead line. Crowden station closed in around 1957 and John Davies, who worked all his life on the railways, lived in a house behind the station.

three

Reservoirs

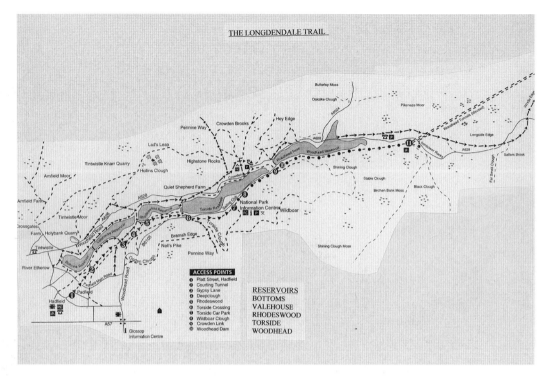

The five reservoirs of the Longdendale Trail which forms part of the Trans-Pennine Trail from Liverpool to Hull.

Opposite: Woodhead reservoir was built between 1848–1877 and is seventy-one feet deep. Here in 1948 Manchester Council waterworks men Tom Mason, Ernie Wood, Harry Leah, Jimmy Thompson and Bill Towers carried tons of stone needed for wall repairs across the water in this small boat. A record shows it took them eight minutes to row each ton load of stone across the water. The edge of Nine Holes Bridge is on the left.

After an inquiry in 1844 into deaths from contaminated water, John Frederick La Trobe Bateman, a civil engineer, was enlisted to advise Manchester & Salford Waterworks Company on new ways of supplying clean water. The water from the Longdendale Valley was seen as the purest so Bateman designed and constructed the five reservoirs in the valley between 1848 and 1877: Woodhead, Torside, Rhodeswood, Valehouse and Bottoms. Water had been used to power mills in the valley but because of the risk of polluting the drinking water many were closed. Some became submerged under the water and others were demolished. The reservoirs rise 344 feet. To accommodate the navvies' families, shanty style huts known as 'New Yarmouths' were built near Rhodeswood. The mile-long Mottram Tunnel was started in 1848 and ran from here to Godley. Thanks to the ingenius Bateman the health of Manchester improved and he went on to do further work at Lake Thirlmere in Cumberland and around thirty other schemes around Great Britain and Ireland. In the year 2000, a blue plaque honouring his achievements was placed on the deepest airshaft of Mottram Tunnel, near Lowry Court in Mottram. At the ceremony were Bateman's great-great-grandchildren, James, John and Kate La Trobe Bateman.

The first Bateman locomotive to run along the water reserves carried workmen and materials. 'The Nibble' electric train was powered by a hydro-electric installation utilising discharge water from Bottoms reservoir and ran up the valley to Crowden from about 1910-1920.

Work was being done on the railway cables at the side of Torside reservoir in the late 1950s. The reservoir, built between 1849-1864, is eighty-four feet deep. In a huge storm in 1901 giant boulders from Wilmer Clough were dislodged and fell around this area. The Glossop & District Sailing Club headquarters moved here from Bottoms Reservoir in 1985.

A 'Bo-Bo,' pulling goods from Penistone en route to Mottram sidings crashed through the buffers on a loop-line at the Torside level crossing in the early hours of April 1957 and caused serious damage to the railside cottage home of Mr and Mrs John Hoderin.

Vale House mill Chimney

Robert Thornley built Vale House cotton mill in around 1790. After the reservoir was completed, it became submerged leaving only the chimney protruding. It became known as the 'Whispering Chimney' because strong winds made whistling noises in it. In 1887 the railway company requested its demolition for safety reasons as passengers were in the habit of crowding to one side of the train to view it.

The Manchester to Sheffield railway line by the side of Torside reservoir. The wonderful scenery of the Longdendale Valley made the journey very enjoyable for those who worked in the city. The express trains made few stops from Manchester and passengers who were a bit slow at opening the doors at Hadfield could find themselves whisked off to Woodhead!

Vale House reservoir in 1966 with views of Hollins Clough, Lad's Leap and Highstones. It was built between 1865-1869 and is forty feet deep. This and Bottoms reservoir were to be used for the storage of storm water and to provide compensation water for the mill owners. In the bad winter of 1947, four workers collapsed from exposure struggling to free a parcel train on the railway near Vale House. In the late 1990's North West Water began the planting of thousands of native saplings by the reservoirs to create new areas of forestry and today the paths around the reservoirs give visitors delightful views without any pollution to the water. The chairman of the Countryside Commission, Sir John Johnson, opened the Longdendale Trail in 1992. The path follows the old railway line and starts close to Hadfield station and provides a level surface for walking and cycling to Woodhead and then it continues as part of the 240 kilometre coast to coast Trans-Pennine Trail from Liverpool to Hull. Lady Towneley, the wife of Lancashire's Lord Lieutenant, formally opened a seven-mile long bridleway from Hadfield to Torside in 1995, which provides circular and linear routes for horse riders.

Left: On the Derbyshire side of Bottom's Reservoir looking out towards Tintwistle is a tunnel under the railway line known locally as the 'Courting Tunnel' but in 1938, when this photograph was taken, this gentleman had only the company of his dog. Nearby are the Deepclough and Higher Deepclough farms.

Below: The dam between Bottoms and Valehouse reservoirs in the 1960s with the village of Tintwistle beyond. It has a capacity to hold 407 million gallons but after the dry summers of the late 1990s reduced water levels exposed peat beds that became so dry there were fires in the reservoir bottom. In 1997 North West Water created a visitor centre for students at the Bottoms depot.

four

Tintwistle

Paradise is a delightful walk by the side of the reservoirs below Tintwistle and near to the villages of Hadfield and Padfield.

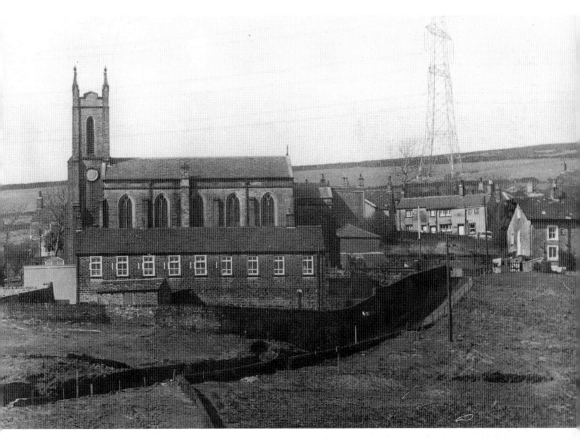

Above: The Norman-style tower of Christ Church built in 1837, alongside village houses built
in the 1960s. A font commemorates local cholera victims and it is reputed that some are buried
in the churchyard as well as at Woodhead chapel. At the time of the Norman Conquest in 1066
'Tingitwistle' formed part of the estate of the Earl of Chester. By 1086 the Domesday survey
spelling was Tengestvisii. In 1621 the name was spelt Tinchtil and Tingetwissel, but to locals it has
for a very long time been known as 'Tinsel'. The name means 'Fork of a river'. At the time of local
government reorganisation, the village moved from Cheshire to Derbyshire. It is roughly eight
thousand feet above sea level. Before the mills were built in the 1750s, handlooms were used in some
of the cottages, examples of which still survive at the eastern end of the village. The population
trebled between 1801-1851. In about 1832 there was a tollhouse where tolls were collected from
travelling traders in flax, yarn and salt and there were eight coaching inns which served the Pennine
travellers between Tintwistle and Saltersbrook. There were three wells in the village at Manchester
Road, New Road and Holy Well, near the border with Crowden and water from the latter was
collected in bottles and taken home to treat whooping cough and arthritis. The local branch
members of the Women's Institute dress this well in the old Derbyshire tradition each year. Tales
abound of Dick Turpin visiting the area with his trusty steed Black Bess.

Opposite below: Bottoms Fountain, seen here in 1954, is a feature created by natural pressure of
waste water overflowing from Bottom reservoir. The fountain can rise to over fifty feet. It was idle
for forty years until water was diverted during flood defence work in 1999. It is now seen again
every time heavy rainwater goes into the overflow channel. Padfield on the Derbyshire side of the
Longdendale Valley can be seen on the horizon.

Tintwistle from Hadfield in 1962. The water, authority buildings and the weir feeding the River Etherow are in the foreground with the tower of Christ Church on the top left and the Independent chapel to the right of the tree. A footpath by the side of the reservoirs starts from the lower left.

Tintwistle Congregational church when it was known as the United Reform church. In 1996 both the Congregational and Christ Church pooled their resources to buy modern children's Bibles for use in Tintwistle's Primary School.

Tintwistle band seen outside their bandroom when it was on New Road, *c.* 1950. They moved to the former Working Men's Club on Old Road in 1995. The village once had three bands, Tintwistle Band of Hope, Tintwistle Temperance and Tintwistle Foresters, which amalgamated around 1888 to form the present band. In 1854 there was also a band called Waterside Brass.

The lamp on the right of Manchester Road was also a drinking fountain and was erected to commemorate the coronation of Edward VII in 1902. A man on the left is walking down the middle of the road, something he wouldn't do in today's traffic! The man on the right is carrying a bucket – was he collecting eggs or going to feed his animals?

The Bulls Head at Tintwistle dates back to 1593 when it was part of a farm. John Hatfield from Crowden Hall was reputedly a regular visitor when returning from his jaunts to Manchester. By the fireplace here in 1950 is owner Mr Tom Rowbottom, a railway signalman who lived on Manchester Road. His family had owned the inn for over 200 years and ale continued to be drawn from the wooden barrels until pumps were installed in 1941.

Mr and Mrs George Garlick, seen here by the door, were the tenants of the Bulls Head in 1950. Legend says that highwayman Dick Turpin often stayed at the pub in the eighteenth century. The taproom has hooks on the ceiling once used by a butcher to hang meat. Around 1900 an elephant stayed in the stables when heavy snow on the Woodhead Pass delayed a circus travelling to Sheffield.

Bottoms Mill, *c.* 1860. This was a cotton-spinning mill built on the Etherow in 1795 by John Turner. In 1865 it was leased to Robert Cross & Co. of Tintwistle. It became known as Bottoms Lodge Mill when the Rhodes Bottom Mill was built in 1836 on the other side of the river.

The Sidebottoms owned Bridge Mill near Tintwistle Bridge on the border with Hadfield and it became part of the Waterside Mill complex in 1855.

Bridge Mill was the scene of a terrible fire in 1899 when many workers lost their jobs subsequently, the council formed a relief committee to help the impoverished. Insurance covered the damage costs and free loaves were distributed to poor families from Tintwisle Conservative Club. The chimney remained in place until 1984.

Waterside Mill and the River Etherow in the 1930s. John Sidebottom bought the mill in 1820 and his son James lived at the Mill House within the complex. A tall obelisk stands outside Christ Church in Tintwistle commemorating the family.

Waterside mill workers at Christmas time in the late 1930s. Waterside was a cotton-spinning mill.

In 1937 ring spinners got fourteen shillings and nine pence a week. Between 1939 and 1945 all the local mills were busy with government orders – many made parachutes.

Waterside mill girls smile for the camera at Christmas. Beatrice Shaw is on the front row, second from the right.

The wedding of Beatrice and Edwin Shaw at St Andrew's church in Hadfield, *c.* 1939. They made their home in Queen Street and had a daughter Freda who became, at a very young age, the organist at Top Chapel in Charlesworth.

Waterside cotton mill sometime after the Second World War. Local firms began to expand after the war and in 1946 there were between 500 and 1,000 jobs unfilled. In 1949 women from Poland, Hungary, Yugoslavia, Lithuania and the Ukraine were attracted into the country to keep the mills running. Many of them married and settled in the area.

Waterside mill later became the factory of Maconochies Foods, Sun-Pat, Rowntree Mackintosh and Nestlés. Other smaller companies have also used parts of the complex. It was famous for a while as the home of Pan Yan Pickle, the aroma of which permeated the air of Tintwistle or Hadfield, depending on the direction of the wind.

This lorry shed its load near Bottoms reservoir when it collided with another in 1960. The emergency services spent two hours releasing one of the trapped drivers as villagers and water workers looked on.

Sexton Street field in the 1960s. The Tintwistle Gala was an annual event where crowds watched the carnival procession in the village followed by sports and activities for children on the gala field. In the background can be seen, on the left, Rhodes Top Mill, in the middle, Padfield and below Castle Hill in the centre is Hadfield. Waterside Mill is on the right.

Arnfield means Eagles Field and Old Arnfield near the Arnfield Reservoir stands close to the busy Trans-Pennine Road out of Tintwistle where the imposing former waterworks building known as Arnfield Tower stands. It was built in 1850 and converted to a Field Centre in 1977 but sadly closed in 1995 due to lack of funds.

Bottoms reservoir below Tintwistle in the 1960s. It was built between 1867-1877 and is forty-eight feet deep. It has been a favourite place for water sports and fishing and with families to play and picnic.

Vivienne Westwood the fashion designer was born Vivienne Isabel Swire in Tintwistle in 1941 and her parents ran the post office. She attended Glossop Grammar School and here at the school bazaar in 1957, in aid of the Amenities Fund, she sold sweets to her teacher Mrs Lawton watched by The Duke of Devonshire who had opened the two-day event.

five

Air
Crashes

Max Wibberley, who was the editor of the *Glossop Chronicle*, is seen here examining the remains of a crashed plane, *c.* 1940. Plane crashes have been common on the moors above the Longdendale Valley and over Glossop. Over 570 crash sites have been researched around the area. Many occurred during the war when inexperienced pilots were flying over unfamiliar terrain but some think the strange lights that have been seen towards Woodhead could also hold the answer to why so many planes have come down. The lights have been described as 'the devil in Longdendale,' 'Boggarts,' 'Will o' the Wisp,' and UFOs. To walkers they appear as bobbing lights of various colours, to the traffic on the A628 they look like the lights of other vehicles. It has been suggested that they are lights from cars on the Snake Road above Glossop as the summit of this road is only about three miles from Shining Clough. In 1996 a television programme in the *Strange But True* series failed to answer the mystery. Lots of wreckage is strewn about the moors serving as a memorial to the various men who died in aeroplanes. The programme showed the Glossop Mountain Rescue Team, donned as Roman Legionaries, marching, as the early armies would have done on their way to Roman forts. Also in 1996 a man in Dinting in Glossop, reported seeing a wedge-shaped unidentified object in the sky in what has become known as the 'Pennine Triangle.' At the same time a Hollingworth man saw something blue-green flash overhead. Wreckage strewn around the moors including badges, buttons, buckles, rings and cartridge cases are still being found. Services remembering the dead are frequently held and enthusiasts regularly go on organised treks in the exposed and dangerous peaks to discover more about the disasters. One of the engines from an Airspeed Oxford that crashed after a map reading exercise in 1945 was brought off the hills and is now displayed in the Heritage Centre in Glossop.

Mr Richard Bridge a rambler from Audenshaw, found RAF bomber L1476 that crashed on Sykes Moss, eighteen hundred feet above sea level and nearly three miles from Torside. The twenty-one-year-old pilots Stanley Robinson and Jack Thomas who had set off from Church Fenton in Yorkshire both died in the accident.

The twin-engine Blenheim bomber hit the ground at about 250 mph creating the water-filled crater in the foreground. Squadron Leader Heber, local police and pressmen were amongst those at the scene here in 1939. Between 1941 and 1948, five other aircraft crashed in the same vicinity.

Wreckage from one of the many crashes in the area. Amongst them was a Lancaster Bomber that crashed near Tintwistle in 1948, a Lysander that crashed above Chew Valley in 1941, a single-seater American aircraft that came down near Charlesworth, Polish pilot Josef Gadowski who crashed near Mottram Church and pilot Ted Rimmer who crashed on hills near Hollingworth.

Opposite above: A Chipmunk that crashed near Arnfield, Tintwistle in July 1951. The pilot Harry Wright, was on a training flight from Barton aerodrome and made a successful escape. Villagers demanded action, wanting a flashing beacon or mast to warn pilots of approaching hills that were often shrouded in thick mist but the mast never appeared.

Opppsite below; A single-engine Beaver L-20, 26145 of the USAF crashed in December 1956 killing its two American crew. It set off from Sculthorpe in Norfolk but never reached Burtonwood air base as it burst into flames and came down on Bramah Edge near Crowden in thick mist. Mr Leslie Simpson, a local railwayman, saw it crash. In the background are Torside reservoir, the railway and Crowden.

Another view of the Beaver that crashed in 1956. Local stonemason, Mr Paul Derbyshire, made a memorial plaque paying tribute to the airmen who died in the Second World War from rock dug in Tintwistle. It was unveiled in 1995 on Bleaklow by Mrs Marion Clifford the ninety-one-year-old mother of one of the pilots.

Another air crash in the valley this time probably from the 1930s but no details are available.

six

Hollingworth

The Arms of Longdendale are based on the coat of arms of the Hollingworths of Hollingworth Old Hall. The holly leaves make reference to their name, the sheaf represents the Earldom of Chester and the lion refers to the arms of Cheshire. Their motto, 'Disce Ferenda Pati' (Learn to endure what must be borne) is fitting to the sometimes-harsh conditions of the valley. The arms, crest and motto can be seen in one of the windows at Mottram church and the family initials are over the north door. The name Hollingworth means 'Holly enclosure.' In the Domesday survey it was known as Holisurde and various spellings have existed, Holynworth, Hollyngworthe and Holinworth. It is reported that Henry Pomfritt, who was a doctor in the village, dealt with over four hundred and fifty accidents at the time of building the Woodhead tunnels; which included fractured skulls, burns and finger amputations. The brass bands of Hollingworth and Tintwistle Foresters combined to play at an open-air sacred musical festival in 1896. The event, attended by 250 people, was held in fields at Crowden to help raise funds for the local school.

Hadfield railway station in 1940 when German prisoners of war and Polish refugees cleared the snow to keep the line open for coal-laden trains from Yorkshire through Woodhead. In 1900 Hollingworth Urban District Council felt the village was missing out on attracting trippers so they asked Grand Central Railways to add 'Hollingworth' to the station sign at Hadfield.

Hollingworth County School Infants in 1929. Fourth from left on the back row is Renee Buxton. Most of the girls were wearing short haircuts with full fringes and most of the boys sitting crossed legged managed to remain still except one on the second row who was kneeling.

Above: The gates of Thorncliff Lodge, Hollingworth, 1952. The creatures were painted by nineteen-year-old Peter Froggatt who lived there. Thorncliff Hall, a Grade II listed building, was the home of mill owner Herbert Rhodes. Thorncliff cottages were known as 'The Dog Kennel'.

Left: The author in her younger days among the daffodils at Millbrook House in 1950. It was once the home of the Sidebottoms who built mills at Millbrook on Hollingworth brook in 1789, at Broadbottom and also developed Waterside Mill in Hadfield. In the winter of 1947 huge snowdrifts blocked the main road at Millbrook between Tintwistle and Hollingworth.

The Revd Maddox greets Sir William and Mrs Clare Lees, who lived at Etherow Lodge, at a garden party at Millbrook House held by Mrs Byrom, who is approaching on the right. There were plans in 1995 to change part of the building into a day nursery but the house has now been converted into private residences.

Etherow House, the former home of mill owner William Sidebottom was demolished in 1953, but the lodge became the home of gardener William (Bill) Sowerbutts seen here at a charity garden party in 1962. He was born into a family of market gardeners who kept poultry on Ashton Moss and were famous for growing celery and other produce which was sold locally. Bill was on the panel of BBC Radio 4's *Gardeners Question Time* for thirty-six years from its start in 1947 the Broadoak Hotel in Ashton. In the year 2000 Professor Stefan Buczacki, former chairman of the same radio programme, unveiled a plaque at the Broadoak in Ashton. Bill's widow, Doris also unveiled a blue plaque honouring her husband (1911-1990) in 2000 at their former home in Hollingworth. It was their wish that the garden would be maintained as a public park. Local residents formed an action group and The Friends of Etherow Lodge Country Park, with aid from the Heritage Lottery and Tameside Council, are working to restore the ten-acre site to its former glory.

Opposite above: Mr Milner, a garden designer at the Crystal Palace, planned the nine-acre gardens of Millbrook House where the Sidebottom family lived up to 1914. From 1924 Franklyn Byrom and his family lived there and every year Mrs E. Byrom held a garden party. In 1949 Ruth, her grandchild, gathered daffodils from the grounds to be sold at the party and raise money for overseas missions.

Opposite below: Chip a dog from Hollingworth suckled two kittens after the mother cat had to be put to sleep in 1961.

Above: The demolition of the Congregational chapel on Taylor Street, Hollingworth in June 1952 as new houses were being built. Below left is Mr Higginbottom working the stone. In the centre and to the right (insets) are close ups of each side of the chapel's stained glass from over the front door.

Opposite above: Local children at the site of the burnt out Hollingworth garage in March 1935. On the left is Sidebottom's Arrowscroft Mill that burnt down in 1982 and was named after the archers who used to practise on the fields here in the 1400s. James Sidebottom retired aged forty-one to pursue his council duties and hobby of weather observation.

Opposite below: A group of local men from Hollingworth look at the wreck of the local clergyman's car, which was burnt when the garage caught fire in 1935.

Right: St Mary's church Gift Day in 1954. It seems that parishioners were happy to come out even in bad weather conditions to add to the collection as Revd Kirk sat for ten hours welcoming them. In 1863 a vicar's wife from Tintwistle, Mrs Katherine Page, collected one shilling a week from Hollingworth people to raise enough money to build St Mary's church which opened in 1864.

Above: The Hollingworth Carnival Queen and her ladies-in-waiting in the 1960s.

Right: The crowning of the Carnival Queen by the retiring queen Alicia Broady in 1966.

Opposite below: After the end of the Second World War there was an increased birth rate for a number of years. Here a local clergyman helps the weighing of the 'Baby Boomers' at a local clinic. Later as class sizes increased, many of the local schools found they needed to extend classrooms to accommodate the extra children.

Members of the Ladies Guild from St Mary's church entered the carnival procession in July 1969. The theme for their float was obviously taken from Lewis Carroll's *Alice's Adventures in Wonderland*.

Workers taking a break from some demolition work in the 1930s. Working clothes in those days were often a suit, including waistcoat with watch fob and chain, clogs, caps and mufflers.

Mersey Mills, known as Rhodes Bottom Mill, was built in Hollingworth in 1859 by the Rhodes family and was demolished in June 1966. In 1950, Webbing Weavers Ltd manufactured narrow webbing from cotton, jute, flax and glass. It formed part of the building known as The Combine, which spread over the River Etherow into Hadfield.

At Easter in 1964 local young people set out from St Mary's church on a sixty-mile pilgrimage, sleeping on the floors of church halls en route to Chester Cathedral where other youth groups from parishes throughout the Chester Diocese joined them for a youth service. Fourth from the left is Roger Goodwin and next to him is Frank Morris.

Olympic Silver medallist Dorothy Shirley signed an autograph for eleven-year-old Lillian Garlic from Hollingworth at Longdendale Road relay race in September 1960.

Philip Scott in typical school uniform of the day, with his father Hollingworth councillor, Harry Scott, at a local old folks party in 1962. They played their accordions at many concerts and functions in the area. Mr Scott worked at Ferrostatics in Glossop and Philip was a boy Scout.

Right: The A628 has become one of the busiest stretches of road in the area with lorries thundering by at all times of the day and night. A lorry near the Gun Inn in Hollingworth hit this bus in 1954. Perhaps the driver was reading the advertising slogan on the back of the bus!

Below: A controversial question facing Longdendale council in November 1962 was whether Hollingworth should have a betting shop. The divisional road engineer had to be convinced that punters parking cars outside the shop would not make the road more dangerous.

A park was created in 1962 at the bottom of Mottram Moor. Mottram church can be seen from its commanding view at the top left. In earlier times a tame short–horned bull judged 'Best in show' on several occasions at Mottram Agricultural Show, used to be paraded down the road to the Gun Inn for all to see.

The junction with Mottram Moor in the 1960s. The Gun Inn, an old coach house on the right, is a Grade II listed building dating back to around 1719. In the 1700s the composer Handel is said to have visited the blacksmith next to the inn and in the 1840s the courthouse was located in the basement.

Pat Phoenix (1924-1986) who played the fiery Elsie Tanner in television's *Coronation Street* lived on Wedneshough Green, a lovely area by the side of the Gun Inn in Hollingworth. The name Wedneshough means 'Valley of Woden,' the Saxon god. Pat's husband was Tony Booth, Prime Minister Tony Blair's father-in-law. Pat and several of her co-stars often made themselves available to open fetes and events in the area.

Above: Mottram men Harry Ward and Hughie Berry in the early 1960s walking by the side of the wall that surrounded the rear of Hollingworth Hall. The Manor House of the Hollingworths was of Edwardian origin but most of the building was from the fifteenth century. During the Wars of the Roses, soldiers marching from Yorkshire, ready to battle with Lancashire were housed here. In the late seventeenth century, the Lords of the Manor held about 690 acres of land including five farms. There was a tradition that the squire and his family went in procession from the hall to St Mary's church, preceded by a tame stag. The estate was sold in 1831 to Robert de Holyngworthe, who was a magistrate, then in 1866 to John Taylor who used it as a school and a mental asylum. It was then sold to Samuel Hadfield at the beginning of the twentieth century. Major Buckley lived there in 1926 then Manchester Corporation bought it for £4,250 and it was finally demolished in 1943. The farm buildings on the left were converted into holiday cottages.

Opposite above: The cottages on Wedneshough Green have changed little over the years. The plaque on Sunny Place a three-storey former weaver's cottage bears the date 1782 and bears the unusual inscription, 'Terms of lease forever'.

Opposite below: The old Albion Mill dated 1859 has now been turned into luxury apartments. In around 1810 the Luddites broke into Wood's Mill nearby and vented their anger by stealing food and destroying machinery.

Above: Landlady Mrs Amy Dutton at the Robin Hood public house on Mottram Moor in 1956, the year it closed. It was originally a farm owned by Lord Tollemache and wheelwrights Seville & Sons once used part of the building. Owned by Wilson's Brewery, the Dutton family had been there since the early 1800s. Both the local botanical society and Mottram Show Committee held their meetings there.

Left: A selection of old leaflets giving details of walking routes and the history of the local area. Visitor centres, information offices and libraries provide details of guided walks from countryside centres and they are also often advertised in the local newspapers.

seven

Mottram

Mottram seen near the Roe Cross Inn in 1965. The name was listed as Motre in the Domesday
Book. The Anglo-Saxon Mot or Moter meant meeting, Ham meant village, and Treum or Rum
meant Tree, so the name seems to mean the place of meeting near a tree. This would seem to fit
with Mottram once being the village where transactions of public business for Stockport and the
Vale of Longden (Longdendale) were conducted. In the reign of Henry II (1154-1189) the manor
of Mottram belonged to the crown. Later it passed between the crown and various people including,
the Earl of Chester, Thomas de Burge, the Earl of Lancaster, Sir Thomas Holland, Lord John Lovel's
family, Sir William Stanley and Richard Wilbraham. By 1692 Lyonel Tollemache inherited the
manors of Mottram and Tintwistle as well as the Lordship of Longdendale. His family retained
the title until it was sold by auction to Tameside MBC in 1987 by the fifth Baron Tollemache of
Helmingham. In July 1995 the MP for Stalybridge and Hyde, Tom Pendry, was presented with the
Lordship of Mottram-in-Longdendale and the Freedom of the Borough of Tameside. Lord Pendry
is the Lord of the Manor until his death when it will revert back to the council. Cheshire County
Council, because of its historic and architectural interest, declared Mottram a conservation area in
1973. There are many listed buildings amongst the millstone grit walls and roofs of stone and blue
welsh slate. Stone from Tintwistle Knarr, a quarry in Tintwistle was used to build Mottram church in
1291.

Known locally as the Deep Cutting, the Mottram Cutting, which leads down into Stalybridge, took twelve years to cut through the 100 yards of solid rock and was completed in 1826 by the Saltersbrook Turnpike Trust. A severe landslide in the 1930s caused the damage seen here in this photograph which was followed by the construction of a new retaining wall. It was necessary to renew the wall again in the 1990s.

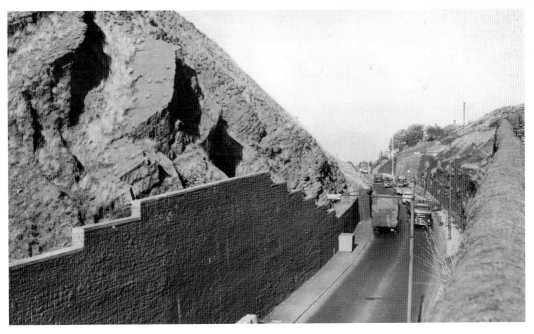

The Deep Cutting in 1961. There is a painted frog in a hollow near the end of the wall on the right. A local story describes how a frog appeared to jump out of the rock when the original road was being cut and the legend lives on in this marker. Others think a frog fossil was found here and still others believe it was probably where a dead frog was found in a crevice in the rock.

Leading off from Stalybridge Road near the Deep Cutting is Hobson Moor Road. At the junction with Dewsnap Lane, a few wooden holiday cottages that were built in the 1930s and 1940s still remain. Further down the lane (seen here on the left) is Higher Lanslow Green Farm where, in 1961, there was a riding school owned by Fred Thompson.

Lumb Farm on Dewsnap Lane. It was built into the hillside and was originally part of the Mottram Hall estate. Mr and Mrs Dawson lowered the floors and dug out the land at the rear to install windows. Mary Dawson married Ned Seaton and lived at Hard Times Farm nearby. Mr Harry Ward (inset) owned the farm from 1958.

Mottram Wakes Week in the 1930s. Crowds from the surrounding areas gathered in August to see the Rush Cart procession on the Monday and various other events throughout the week culminating with the Trail Hunt on land off Ashworth Lane. The bookmakers always did a brisk trade. Both Faircloughs and Meschias can be seen selling ice cream from horse-drawn carts.

The last Trail Hunt was in 1939 and prize money varied from fifteen shillings to £5. On this occasion, Roland Firth was the starter, J. Swindells was the judge and Major Bett was the veterinarian. After the three-mile race to test their stamina, it was traditional to feed the dogs with a currant cake and port wine.

Mottram Old Hall was occupied by the Hollingworth family from the fourteenth to the eighteenth centuries. The front was changed in 1825 when Captain Hadfield lived there. After 1914, the hall was turned into a convalescence hospital for wounded soldiers and staffed by Red Cross nurses. Today it is a private residence and Mottram Agricultural Show uses the land for its annual event.

Mottram Old Hall Lodge. In the grounds there was a monument bearing the inscription, 'A tribute of respect, erected to the memory of George Hadfield who died at Old Hall and was buried at Glossop in 1831. He was proprietor of Old Hall, Thorncliff Hall and other estates and by his superior abilities and persevering exertions he brought them to their present state of completeness.'

Mr Gould of Hollingworth in 1930 when his bull won best in show. The show began in 1904 when local farmers raised £5 to stage a cattle fair around the Crown Pole in Market Street. As interest grew, the fair turned into a show and by 1909 it was known as The Mottram & District Agricultural Society.

Mottram show has also been held on land off Ashworth Lane and also on land off Hyde Road before the Hattersley housing estate was built. Two of the show officials in the 1950s were Mr J. Jackson (left) and the president, Mr William Allen, who was also a local councillor.

Above: This small boy entered his pet rabbit and won the 'Fur Fancier' cup in 1961 at Mottram Agricultural Show. As the show grew it included sections for produce, cookery and flower arranging. Sheep dog handling and displays from various groups have always made the show entertaining.

Left: Pauline Le Mar from Charlesworth on her horse called Foxy was one of the show jumpers at the 1958 show. The popular show held at Easter time was mostly a gymkhana and the main show was held in August. The show is now held at the May Bank Holiday and also in August.

Right: Four-year-old Alison Pickin, from Charlesworth, was a competitor in the leading rein class at the Easter Monday show in March 1967. All entries received a chocolate egg even if they failed to win any other prizes. Mottram church is visible in the background.

Below: Mr Leonard Hartley from Ashton does a lap of honour after receiving prizes in the late 1940s when the show was held off Ashworth Lane, Mottram. An all-weather stand advertising the local papers was very popular especially in inclement weather.

Laurence Stephen (L.S.) Lowry (1887-1976) at an arts and crafts exhibition in 1964. The well-known artist was born in Trafford Park and moved to Pendlebury in 1909. By 1915 he was attending evening classes at Manchester College of Art and Salford School of Art whilst working as a rent collector, clerk, bookkeeper and cashier, which he did until retirement. It was from his observations of the working class that he got his inspiration to create the thin men in his paintings. He moved to The Elms on Stalybridge Road in Mottram in 1948, where local lady Mrs Bessie Swindles was his housekeeper. As a small child I can remember visiting his home with my father who was taking photographs of the artist at work. The easel, floor and his suit were all splattered with paint. There was a large wooden cabinet filled with books and pieces of crockery in one corner and at the side was a cardboard box containing smaller books. The room was lit by one single light bulb as he worked on the painting entitled 'Open Space', depicting Oldham market. At his fifth exhibition in 1951, he had forty pictures on show at the Lefevre Gallery in London. He painted and sketched still life, seascapes and churches but was most famous for his matchstick-men pictures. He also enjoyed classical music. His work was not recognised until 1939 and he once said; 'I wonder what they will think of me when I'm gone'. The 'Art of Lowry' was staged at the Royal Academy in 1976 and attracted 180,216 visitors. Manchester City Art Gallery recreated his studio and sitting room and Salford Art Gallery staged an exhibition to mark the centenary of his birth in 1987. His reputation has not only spread around Britain but also internationally. His work has been honoured with doctorates, the Freedom of Salford, the publishing of several books and with The Lowry galleries and theatre at Salford Quays which was built in 1997 and officially opened by the Queen in 2000. It is a great pity he never saw this great tribute. He once said he'd worked like a slave but the pictures would speak for themselves and he'd be judged by what he'd done. He was for many people locally a familiar and lonely-looking figure as he stood near the traffic lights in Mottram waiting for the Manchester bus, wearing his familiar long coat with the collar turned up and wearing a trilby hat.

Right: 'The Wren' which L.S. Lowry painted from a photograph of Kathleen Leatherbarrow, the daughter of friends in Pendlebury who invited him for meals. He took the thirteen-year-old to a pantomime in 1940 and despite many offers for the painting it remained in his home with the original photograph until his death.

Below: At the age of sixty-eight Mr Lowry was elected Associate of the Royal Academy. Longdendale Rural District Council recognised this achievement by presenting him with an illuminated address at the Court House in Mottram in 1956. He replied with these words, 'I greatly appreciate what you have done this evening, I will never forget your action, thank you'.

Left: Lowry never married but Cllr Mrs J. Williamson here managed to bring a twinkle to Lowry's eye at an event in 1956. Tameside Council's Blue Plaque to his memory says, '....to this famous North Country artist of The Elms, Stalybridge Road, Mottram, which was his home from 1948 till his death in 1976. Lowry's paintings document the lives of ordinary communities in the industrial Northwest'.

Below: This runaway steamroller crashed into the gates of the police station at the junction of Mottram Moor and Back Moor in 1951. John Evans, the son of the sergeant, was evidently pleased that it hadn't crushed his pedal car which had been parked close by. The building is now a private house.

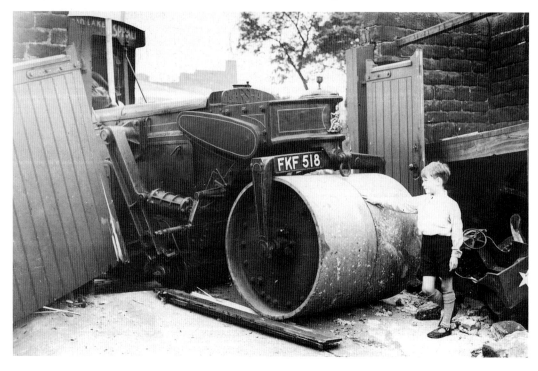

Above: The Savoy cinema on Mottram Moor closed in 1957. The building was condemned in 1962 but was still standing in 1968. The sound of rain on the roof often drowned out the sound of films and when it was warm the place developed an unpleasant smell so it was nicknamed the 'Bug Hut'. William Ford House for the elderly was later built near-by.

Below: This smithy was built in about 1836 to cater for the increase in stagecoach traffic following the opening of Captain Hyde Clarke Mottram New Road the previous year. Before that time the route from Mottram to Hyde was via Hattersley. Tom Philips is seen here trimming the hooves of Pilot and working at the anvil in 1949 (inset). Later, Malcolm Manifold became the blacksmith and farrier.

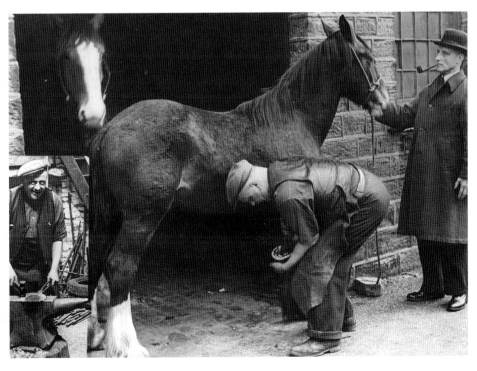

Above: Seven whales of various sizes and weighing over nine tons came to the village in May 1950 en route to W. Hey & Sons, a processing plant for fertilisers and oils in Mottram. Over one hundred had been washed ashore at Dunbar in Scotland and, as the weather was warm, local people were keen to see them removed before they became a hazard!

Left: Prince Philip, the Duke of Edinburgh, in a limousine travelling through Mottram on his way to Manchester Airport in March 1964. He had been to Hyde, Dukinfield and Stalybridge on an industrial visit. Local ladies out shopping got soaked waiting in the rain for a glimpse of him as he passed.

Opposite above: Patricia Gerrard Cooke lived in Mottram and taught art at Altrincham Grammar School. She is seen here on the left as a 23-year-old in front of a painting of the girls from the school. This was one of her works of art which was staged at an exhibition in Hyde Festival Hall in 1959.

Opposite below: Mr and Mrs Marsland and family, *c.* 1960. Mr Marsland had a butcher's shop on Market Street in Mottram near to the White Hart Inn. He also bred Pembrokeshire Corgi dogs whose pedigree names all contained the local name of War Hill.

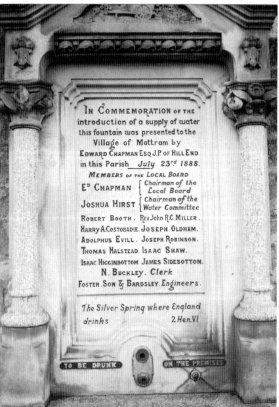

IN COMMEMORATION OF THE
introduction of a supply of water
this fountain was presented to the
Village of Mottram by
EDWARD CHAPMAN ESQ J.P OF HILL END
in this Parish _July 23rd 1888._
MEMBERS OF THE LOCAL BOARD

ED CHAPMAN	Chairman of the Local Board
JOSHUA HIRST	Chairman of the Water Committee

ROBERT BOOTH. REV JOHN R.C. MILLER.
HARRY A. COSTOBADIE. JOSEPH OLDHAM.
ADOLPHUS EVILL. JOSEPH ROBINSON.
THOMAS HALSTEAD. ISAAC SHAW.
ISAAC HIGGINBOTTOM JAMES SIDEBOTTOM.
N. BUCKLEY. Clerk
FOSTER. SON & BARDSLEY. Engineers.

_The Silver Spring where England
drinks_   _2 Hen. VI_

TO BE DRUNK   ON THE PREMISES

Above: Market Street, *c.* 1900. The Crown Pole on the left was erected on the village green to commemorate the coronation of George III in 1760. The court house, behind, was a petty session's court presided over by Captain Hollyngworthe. In this court a certain Mr Arundale from Hattersley was sentenced to transportation for the crime of stealing wages from a Broadbottom mill.

Left: Edward Chapman of Hill End House presented this fountain in front of the Old Court House in 1888. It commemorates the introduction of a water supply to Mottram. The court house has also been used as a library, an information office and an office for the Tameside Patrollers.

Children playing at the village green in 1954. Harold Chapman, a JP from Hillend House near Broadbottom, replaced the original wooden Crown Pole with a metal one in 1926. In 1974 Mottram was twinned with Ruppichteroth 900km away in Germany and the town's name was added to the direction signs. The Pack Horse Inn is in the background.

Above: Each year in July, villagers gathered at the Crown Pole for the Mottram Sing. On the right are twins dressed in their Sunday best in this view of 1949. In the week preceding the Sing it was traditional for people equipped with buckets containing bleach, donkey stones and scrubbing brushes to clean the gravestones behind the church at the top of Church Brow.

Left: Canon M. Power is seen here in 1940 making his sermon after the hymn singing. He was well known for his forthright sermons and on this occasion condemned drunkenness and as it was wartime, admonished the crowds for the over use of pleasure trips and wasting petrol too!

Left: Mr W. Andrew, resplendent with watch chain and holding a foal, on land behind the Pack Horse Inn in October 1955 when he retired as landlord after thirty-six years. He was the trail-hunt secretary until it finished in 1939.

Below: The demolition of the old stables at the Pack Horse Inn in 1962 to make room for a car park. The inn gets its name from the pack horse trains that passed this way from Salters Brook. For many years the mobile trailer library parked here, getting power from an electricity bollard on the car park.

Left: Across the road from the inn stood a row of four cottages that were demolished in 1963. The original smithy was also on this side of the road before it was transferred to a fenced off area in front of the Pack Horse Inn. The church tower protrudes above the rooftops.

Below: The Old School House in the 1950s. Over the door are the words, 'Manners maketh man' and over the window, dated 1862, are the words, 'Come ye children, harken to me. I will teach you the fear of the Lord, the beginning of wisdom. Bring them up in the nurture and admonition of the Lord'.

Left: The row of cottages below the church were built into the hillside and needed modernisation but were demolished in around 1963. In their place, the council provided seats and a garden in 1966. A blue plaque honouring Mottram man Sir Edmund Shaa, who funded the church tower, was placed at the top of the steps. The building just visible on the right is the old mortuary.

Below: Cllr Warhurst opened Mottram Recreation Ground on Broadbottom Road in 1937. It is seen here in 1962 when plans had been announced to develop the site with housing. On the left is the vicarage and the houses to the right are on Ashworth lane. The Wakes fun fair with the big wheel, candy floss and side-shows came here throughout the 1950s. In 1977 Tameside Council built the new library to replace the trailer library.

The last Longdendale Rural District Council, *c.* 1974. Back row, left to right: R. Taylor (surveyor), Cllrs N. Burgess and J. Saville, W.W. Sargent (clerk), H.K. Walker (treasurer), Cllrs B.E. Singleton and A. Mercer, F. Skirrow (chief public health officer). Front row, left to right: Cllrs T. Langford, D.E. Green, S.F. Ellison, W.J. Shaw, K.W. Shaw, S.R. Oldham (leader of Tameside MBC), E. Greenfield.

Seventeen-year-old Miss Jean Wood from the hardware store on Mottram Moor was chosen as Miss Northwest area Young Conservative Queen for 1965-1966.

Mottram Community Centre on Church Brow, held a Guy Fawkes Hot Pot supper in 1962. The building was originally a school built in 1832 which had its iron railings removed to melt down for salvage during the war. In 1995 Longdendale Amenity Society had new ones made to match the originals.

The sundial outside the church was once a cross, which had stood there since 1760. It was made by Ralph Wardleworth, a teacher at the Old Grammar School, on the left, and was restored in 1897 for Queen Victoria's Diamond Jubilee. On the right is Mottram Primary School. The area is known as War Hill after a battle here in 1138.

A Grade II listed building, the church of St Michael and All Angels stands 750 feet above sea level and is known as the Cathedral of East Cheshire because of its position. It dates from 1291 being built in memory of soldiers who died during the battle on War Hill but the present building dates from the fifteenth century.

The interior of the church decorated for Easter with lilies and palm leaves and the alabaster pulpit on the left in the 1930s. The piers and chancel arch are original the rest was renovated in 1854. There are bread racks dated 1619 and 1737 on either side of the north door from which food was distributed to the poor.

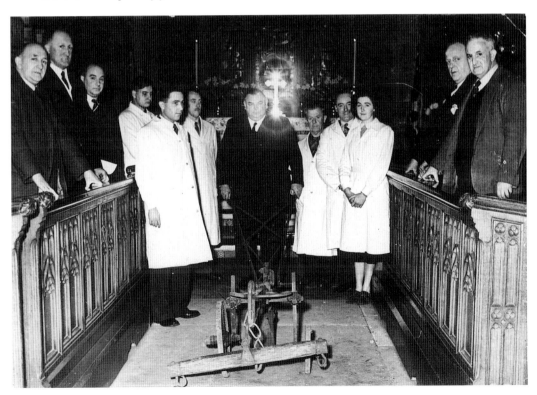

Right: The church has a twelfth-century stone barrel font mounted on a millstone from Brectomley Mill in Hattersley. It was once used as a rainwater butt. The church has two chapels built with the aid of endowments from the Hollingworth and Staley families. The Staley Chapel became the private chapel of the Chapman family.

Below: Plough Sunday was held each year at the church to offer the work in the farmer's fields to God. The officials from the agricultural society in January 1955 were, from left to right, L. Boden, I. Maben, E. Brierley, D. Brierley, W. Crowton, W. Booth, W. Mansfield, C. Barnett, J. Bowers, Edith Walton, N. Philips and J. Jackson.

Ivor Jones and Brian Scarborough installed a new mechanism for Mottram church clock in 1952. The old clock was 190 years old and was the third one in the tower. It came from Arden Park in Bredbury, Stockport. Underneath the dial is one of the handles that was used to wind the clock before it had an electric winder.

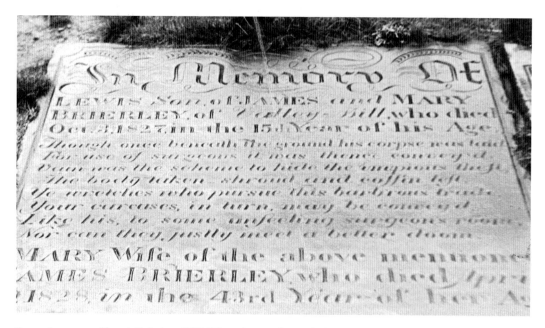

From the grave of Lewis Brierley, 1827, 'Though once beneath the ground his corpse was laid for use of surgeons. Vain was the scheme to hide the impious theft. The body taken shroud and coffin left. The wretches, who pursue this barbarous trait, your carcasses may be conveyed to some unfeeling surgeon's room. Nor can they, justly meet a better doom.'

Right: The parish church from the grounds of Old Hall. Other denominational churches in Mottram have been Methodist, Congregational and Unitarian. The Unitarian church on Hyde Road opened in 1846. It closed in 1995 and was converted into flats. The Congregational on Stalybridge Road was originally rented from the Methodists and is now the Evangelical Church.

Below: The Mottram stocks were unearthed three feet below ground near Chain Bar Lane in Hattersley when the Manchester overspill estate was started in the early 1960s. They are thought to be 400 years old and were erected near the Crown Pole in 1968 by Longdendale council chairman, Mr J. Mills.

The Old Grammar School was for the sons of wealthy landowners until 1832 when a new school was built on Church Brow. When this closed, scholars were transferred back to the old building. During the Second World War the Civil Defence used it. After the war it became a shirt and pyjama factory and later it was extended and became Mottram Primary School.

The Old Post Office Farm was where the Wagstaff family lived for over 200 years as blacksmiths, farmers and postmasters. In 1796 a barn was converted into a cotton factory. Members of the Wagstaff Society met in 1995 at the Pack Horse Inn in Mottram to share their genealogy. The former prime minister John Major's wife Norma and Florence Nightingale were both Wagstaffs.

Three residents of Mottram in the 1950s. They are, from left to right: Mrs Hannah Manifold, Mrs Monks and Miss Polly Wild. Hannah lived at Pingot Farm in Hattersley and later lived with her sister Polly on Broadbottom Road. Their friend Mrs Monks lived in the cottages near to the Junction Inn on Market Street and later moved to Royton.

The Waggon and Horses, seen here in 1958, changed its name to the Waggon in 1982. Landlord Kenneth Charlesworth used to have the covered waggon floodlit. In the eighteenth century it was a farm and the area was known as Woodside. Broadbottom Road was built in 1858 for the use of horse-drawn waggons transporting stone to construct the railway at Broadbottom.

Four generations of two Longdendale families met at a wedding in 1952. They are, back row, left to right: Raymond Armitage, Doris Preston, Raymond, Stanley and Raymond (jnr) Manifold. Middle, left to right: Kathleen Higginbottom, Kathy Preston, Edith Armitage, Minnie and Barry Manifold, Hannah Manifold. Front, left to right: baby Raymond Armitage, Brian Preston and Roy Manifold.

Harold Chapman, Master of the Beagle Hunt outside his home, Hill End House in the early years of the twentieth century. The Chapmans were a wealthy Longdendale textile family; John became the lord of the manor at Mottram. During the cotton famine, he set up a soup kitchen at his home which was originally a yeoman farmhouse built in 1604.

eight

Broadbottom

Col. William Sidebottom (1842-1933) with his collection of prize-winning silver, *c.* 1930. He lived at Harewood Lodge, Broadbottom with his sister Lucy and six servants. He became a town councillor and was MP for High Peak and colonel of the Volunteer Defence. He was a director of the Grand Central Railway. He gave a house in King Street to the Young Men's Club for billiards and as a reading room, which stayed open until the 1960s. The Grade II-listed Harewood Lodge was recently restored and offered for sale (at the time of writing) for over a quarter of a million pounds. Many houses have now been built in the grounds of the lodge.

In the time of Edward III, there was a local family with the name Broadbottom who held land in the area. Broadbottom was on the south side of the township of Mottram with only a few inhabitants at Botham Hall, Broadbottom Hall and on a few farms. William de Brodebothum lived at Broadbottom Hall in the early 1300s and the Wolegh's in the latter part of that century. Later occupants were the Bostocks who owned the village up to the 1800s. Joseph Sidebottom, of a local mill owning family, built Harewood Lodge in 1847. Lord Tollemache, the lord of the manor owned Gorsey Brow, The Hague and the Hodge. The River Etherow, which runs through the Wood at Bottoms Hall, provided power for the mills here. From the eighteenth century it powered Moss Mill, a woollen and later cotton mill. Other mills in the area included Broad Mills, Lymefield, Besthill, West End, Moss Mill and Hodge Lane Printworks. In earlier times, pack horses carried wool and salt over the Pennines coming down from Chisworth, crossing the Etherow via Stirrups Farm, before continuing up Hurst Clough brook to Hill End Lane and over the Mudd to Mottram church. The historic Besthill pack horse bridge, built in 1683 over the Etherow on Lower Market Street, divides Broadbottom from its Derbyshire neighbours, Charlesworth and Chisworth.

Above: Thomas Henry Buxton in the greenhouse at Harewood Lodge in the 1930s. He was the superintendent at St Andrew's church mission in Hadfield and Col. Sidebottom was an active member of the Anglican church committee so perhaps he was visiting the colonel on church business.

Right: A path in Bothams Hall Wood. The hall that once stood in this area was built in the seventeenth century and the river Etherow formed a horse shoe bend between here and Leyland Farm. The eighteen-mile Cown Edge Way from Hyde, descends from Werneth Low to Botham's Hall, Boarfold, Chew Wood, Charlesworth and ends in Hazel Grove.

David Grassing of Market Street was a television sound supervisor in Manchester and built this boat out of old scenery from the set of *Coronation Street* and launched it at Marple in 1963. Coincidentally, Julie Hesmondhalgh, who plays Hayley Cropper in *Coronation Street* made Broadbottom her home.

There was a time in the 1960s when it was fashionable again for ladies to wear hats and these two were modelling them for a show put on by 'Lucie's of Hyde' held at Broadbottom Methodists chapel on School Brow in 1967. The event raised £13 for charity.

Above: Broadbottom's old sewage lakes were enlarged as the new Hattersley housing estate was built and here Sir Wesley Pemberton, the chairman of Cheshire County Council unveils a plaque commemorating the start of this new phase of construction in 1964. The pipes from Hattersley went through Great Wood under the tollery, a terrace of land near Hurst Clough where spoil from the old Hattersley railway tunnel had been deposited.

Right: June Taylor was an information assistant at Lymefield Visitor Centre in 1995 when a maze was planted as a visitor attraction. The centre was opened in 1988 and promotes guided walks and activities for all ages. Lymefield Mill was built in 1861 and became a carpet mill after the war, later being used for screen-printing. Nearby is the Lymefield Garden centre and tea-rooms.

New track being laid near Broadbottom station in the 1940s. Servicemen in uniform are amongst those working and the two men in trilby hats appear to be supervising. Prisoners of war had been used to clear snow from the railway lines during the war.

A new section of track being laid near the station at Broadbottom. In the 1840s, a railway worker called Ford was transported for the murder of a Broadbottom gamekeeper called Shaw. In the 1960s, a Wild West film set, known as Constock, was created near Broadbottom viaduct by the Manchester Fast Gun Club for amateur film makers to shoot *A Man Called Slade*.

nine

Charlesworth
and
Chisworth

Broadbottom railway viaduct, seen here in 1961, is a Grade II-listed structure, stands 138 feet over the River Etherow and is 555 feet long. It was opened in 1842 for the Sheffield, Ashton & Manchester Railway. The stone supports are original but the brick pillars replaced timber supports in 1859. Besthill Bridge carries traffic from Cheshire into Derbyshire and was opened in June 1949.

On the Derbyshire side of the river at the lower end of Long Lane, was a row of brick houses nicknamed New York after three families living there in the early twentieth century emigrated to America to escape the cotton famine.

In 1308, Robert de Charlesworth gave eight acres of arable land in Charlesworth to the Welsh abbot of Basingwerke. The monks are thought to have established a farm here and built a chapel dedicated to Mary Magdalene. Cown Edge and Coombs rocks, where the druid remains Tumulus and Robin Hood's Picking Rods can be found, surrounding the village, which stands next to Chisworth. From Monks Road, an old salt trail, there are wonderful views of the Longdendale valley, the Pennine hills, Manchester airport and, on a clear day, the Welsh hills. It was from here that the abbots collected rents from the Glossop estate on a block of stone known as the Abbot's Chair. They chose this spot because it is about the same distance from Hayfield, Charlesworth and Glossop. Found nearby was a block of millstone grit thought to be the base stone from an old cross. Charlesworth used to have a cattle fair in April and Wednesday markets. Also, a fair at the festival of St Mary Magdalene was granted in 1328. St Mary's chapel was once a place of worship for Independent Calvinists.

After the Manchester blitz, many families moved here for a new life in the country but some returned to the city after the experience of having to struggle through snowdrifts each winter to reach the station to get to work. Broadbottom's New York was demolished in 1961 giving a clearer view from this point of the viaduct, the Methodist chapel and the houses on Gorsey Brow.

Storry Witty & Co Ltd from Beverley made paint, putty, whiting and ferramastic. In 1960 one of the company lorries carrying a fifteen-ton load failed to make it up Long Lane and then ran backwards into a row of houses. Only minutes earlier, a mother had called in her two young children who had been playing next to the baby in the pram. This area is now a car park.

Young admirers of newly hatched chicks at Le Mar's poultry farm on Long Lane Charlesworth in the spring of 1954.

Above: St John's church Charlesworth, at the top end of Long Lane, celebrated its centenary in October 1949. To mark the occasion, the parish church was floodlit.

Left: Pauline Le Mar and her new husband, married at St John's church, Charlesworth, in the 1960s.

During the war, women's groups were set up to sew and knit socks, mittens and balaclava hats for troops and prisoners of war. Charlesworth's women are seen here in the Liberal Hall in 1940. Not only were they encouraged to 'make do and mend' but also to 'keep a pig 'and guard against 'careless talk'.

Almost camouflaged against a highly patterned sofa are a family of cats and a rabbit which happily lived together at a Charlesworth farm in the 1950s. Rabbits as well as cats can be trained to use litter trays.

Opposite above: A Rose Queen from one of the local Sunday schools with her attendants in the early 1960s. They stopped to sing a hymn on Glossop Road, Charlesworth, at the annual Whit Walk procession.

Opposite below: Isolated farms at Charlesworth in December 1965. In the background are Coombs Rocks. In 1996, local councillors sought to add several landmarks to this designated conservation area. They included Well Head Farm and Church Brow and the disused quarry near Boggard Lane.

Right: The Revd V. Newman at Charlesworth Independent Chapel in February 1961. Along with four others he re-painted the walls. The present chapel, known locally as Top Chapel, was built in 1795. The graveyard is built on a bed of rock and consequently most of the graves are unusually shallow. In 1954 fifteen-year-old Pearl Tetlow was the organist.

Below: Mr Weston from Glossop Road in Charlesworth was a prolific local artist and is seen here in his living room with a display of his paintings in the 1960s. He was a member of the Glossop artist's group.

Artist L.S. Lowry was the guest of honour at Charlesworth Women's Institute arts and crafts exhibition in 1964. Cllr Brenda Tetlow, on the right, served for more than fifty years in local government and represented the village of Charlesworth from 1974. She was elected as High Peak's first mayor in 1974 after battling to keep Charlesworth in Derbyshire.

Mrs Robertson, L.S. Lowry, Mrs B. Tetlow (a founder member of the village WI), Mr Robertson and Mr Attwood take afternoon tea at Charlesworth's art's and crafts exhibition in 1964.

Looking resplendent in their best Sunday clothes are scholars from Chisworth Wesleyan School with their teacher in the 1920s.

At Chisworth Methodist day school's Bring and Buy Sale in July 1962, the infant and junior department percussion band raised £17 for their efforts. Even the ones who only got to play triangles seem just as happy as they pick out the beat to 'Clip-clip-clop'. Revd A. Snell was the chairman and Mrs A. Bradley opened the event.

Other local titles published by Tempus

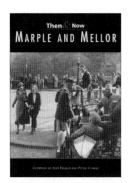

Marple and Mellor
ANN HEARLE AND PETER CLARKE

This book contains over ninety old photographs of Marple and Mellor each carefully matched with photographs of the same scenes taken today. They show all aspects of the life in the area; street scenes, schooldays, industrial life and leisure times, a treat for all who know and love these old neighbouring communities.
07524 2644 3

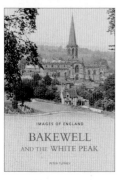

Bakewell and the White Peak
PETER TUFFREY

This book contains a fascinating selection of over 200 old photographs of this much visited area of north Derbyshire. Centred on the market town of Bakewell the book is composed almost entirely from photographs taken by the well known photographer E.L. Scrivens in the first half of the twentieth century. It will delight and stimulate pleasant memories for anyone who grew up in or has been a regular visitor to the Peak District.
07524 3042 4

Glossop: Volume Two
SUE HICKINSON AND MICHAEL BROWN

In this second volume of old photographs of Glossop produced by Tempus the authors have selected a fascinating sequence of images that successfully conjure up a time gone by in this important north Derbyshire mill town. The book will be enjoyed by all who know and love Glossop.
07524 3286 9

Prehistory in the peak
MARK EDMONDS AND TIM SEABORNE

Fifty years ago the Peak District was designated a National Park , the first to be recognised as such in the country. The area is one rich in prehistoric monuments and this book shows the reader how to look for and recognise evidence of the Peak's ancient past. It is about how land and society have changed in step with one another; changes in vegetation, use, ownership and perception. The book explores how Derbyshire's ancient monuments appear to us today and what they may have meant to people in the past.
07524 1483 6

If you are interested in purchasing other books published by Tempus, or in case you have difficulty finding any Tempus books in your local bookshop, you can also place orders directly through our website
www.tempus-publishing.com